Dedicated to

_____

with love from

_____

This journal was started on

_____

"MOTHER *is the name for God*
in the lips and hearts of CHILDREN."

—William Makepeace Thackeray

CONTENTS

Celebrating the special bond between
mothers and daughters, this journal is a place to collect
your thoughts about each other, and about yourself.

＊＊＊

For mothers, this book will help you record your thoughts
and memories of one of the most basic and complex
relationships in your life. It will help your daughter
understand the dreams you hold for her life, and for yours.

＊＊＊

For daughters, this book can help your mother better
understand the person she has raised.

＊＊＊

Together, this journal can help build a stronger bond and
more enduring bridge between generations and friends.

home

"*Home is not where you* LIVE
       but where they UNDERSTAND *you.*"

–Christian Morgenstern

HOME

There is a place that is as much

a physical one as a state of mind.

We call that place "home."

It is the center of our lives,

where traditions are born,

and families are nurtured.

HOME

What makes a happy home:

HOME

What I like best about our home:

_____

_____

_____

_____

_____

_____

_____

What I like least about our home:

_____

_____

_____

_____

_____

_____

_____

HOME

The room I feel most "at home" in:

Words I use to describe our home:

HOME

The best party we ever threw was:

Our most memorable guest:

HOME

Projects we like to do together:

The best parts of working on projects together:

HOME

Our most treasured heirlooms:

Why we treasure these things:

HOME

Things I would like to pass on to my children:

HOME

Our family's most important traditions:

Our family's most fun traditions:

HOME

My favorite holiday:

Why it's my favorite:

HOME

What holidays mean to me:

_____

_____

_____

_____

_____

_____

Favorite family traditions:

_____

_____

_____

_____

_____

_____

_____

_____

HOME

My favorite family recipes: _____

_____

_____

_____

_____

_____

_____

I learned the recipe from: _____

_____

_____

_____

_____

_____

_____

_____

HOME

Things we celebrate every year:

Things our family does at least once every year:

A Picture's Worth

A Picture's Worth

BELIEFS

& dreams

"I have a simple PHILOSOPHY.
Fill what's empty. Empty what's full.
And SCRATCH *where it itches."*

–Alice Roosevelt Longworth

BELIEFS AND DREAMS

We live our lives by the light of certain guiding principles.

These principles chart the path our life will follow,

but it is our dreams that propel us.

BELIEFS AND DREAMS

Dreams that have come true:

BELIEFS AND DREAMS

My dreams for you:

BELIEFS AND DREAMS

My dreams for you and I, together:

BELIEFS AND DREAMS

What I most want to see that I have not seen yet:

The things I most want you to see in your lifetime:

BELIEFS AND DREAMS

The best age to be is: _____ *because:* _____

BELIEFS AND DREAMS

Things worth fighting for:

Beliefs and Dreams

Things worth volunteering time to:

Things worth donating money to:

BELIEFS AND DREAMS

Personal battles:

31

BELIEFS AND DREAMS

My personal motto:

BELIEFS AND DREAMS

A fulfilled life has to include:

BELIEFS AND DREAMS

Turning points in my life:

BELIEFS AND DREAMS

The most meaningful places in my life:

BELIEFS AND DREAMS

My superstitions:

BELIEFS AND DREAMS

Things I know for sure:

BELIEFS AND DREAMS

Things I want you to know about men:

Beliefs and Dreams

What one should seek in a life partner:

BELIEFS AND DREAMS

My good habits:

My bad habits:

A Picture's Worth

A Picture's Worth

A Picture's Worth

relationships

"If a child is to keep alive an inborn sense of WONDER without
any such gift from the fairies, she needs the companionship of one
adult who can share it, rediscovering with her the joy, excitement
and MYSTERY of the world we live in."

                                                    –RACHEL CARSON

RELATIONSHIPS

A hand to guide us, a hand to support us,

or a hand simply to hold.

Hand in hand, we walk through the world together.

RELATIONSHIPS

The women who preceded us in our family:

Great Grandmothers:

Grandmothers:

Mothers:

RELATIONSHIPS

In my family, I take after:

RELATIONSHIPS

Namesakes in our family:

Why our namesakes were memorable:

RELATIONSHIPS

Where my mother was born:

When my mother was born:

RELATIONSHIPS

Where my daughter was born:

When my daughter was born:

RELATIONSHIPS

Characteristics of a good mother: _____

_____

_____

_____

_____

_____

_____

_____

_____

_____

_____

_____

_____

_____

_____

_____

_____

_____

RELATIONSHIPS

Characteristics of a good daughter:

Relationships

Ingredients for a good relationship:

RELATIONSHIPS

What a good friend is especially good at:

How a real friend makes you feel:

RELATIONSHIPS

The most influential person in my life:

What I learned from them:

RELATIONSHIPS

How my mother has helped me grow:

Relationships

How my daughter has helped me grow:

RELATIONSHIPS

The things I want you to learn from me:

RELATIONSHIPS

The things I love most about you:

RELATIONSHIPS

How you're different from anyone else I've ever met:

RELATIONSHIPS

Our nicknames for each other:

Relationships

The greatest gift I ever received from you was:

When I received it from you, I felt:

Relationships

The greatest gift I ever gave to you was:

When I gave it to you, I felt:

RELATIONSHIPS

The greatest gift we, together, gave to another was:

_____

_____

_____

_____

_____

_____

When we gave it, we felt:

_____

_____

_____

_____

_____

_____

_____

_____

RELATIONSHIPS

Ways in which we are alike:

Ways in which we are different:

Relationships

My greatest strengths:

Your greatest strengths:

RELATIONSHIPS

Ways we can improve ourselves:

RELATIONSHIPS

How you've changed my life:

How I've changed your life:

A Picture's Worth

A Picture's Worth

A Picture's Worth

memories

"*In* MEMORY, *everything seems to happen to* MUSIC."

–Tennessee Williams

Memories

Our mind's eye is like a camera,

gathering memories of life.

And, when we look through these snapshots,

we are reminded of what a magical camera — and life — it is.

MEMORIES

Earliest memory of my mother:

Earliest memory of my daughter:

MEMORIES

Things I regret doing:

Things I regret not doing:

MEMORIES

My best childhood memories:

My best friend growing up:

MEMORIES

My best date ever:

My worst date ever:

MEMORIES

My most peaceful memory:

MEMORIES

My best day ever:

MEMORIES

My best moment: ---

MEMORIES

How I want to be remembered:

A Picture's Worth

A Picture's Worth

PLAYING

favorites

"If children grew up according to early INDICATIONS, *we should have nothing but* GENIUSES."

–GOETHE

PLAYING FAVORITES

Atop every list there is a favorite –

the standard by which all others are judged.

Never stop searching until you find the best that life has to offer,

and, never settle for less.

Playing Favorites

Favorite childhood toy:

Favorite time of day:

Favorite season of the year:

Favorite ice cream flavor:

Favorite candy:

Favorite flower:

Favorite color:

Playing Favorites

Favorite aroma:

What it reminds me of:

PLAYING FAVORITES

Favorite restaurant:

What I order there:

PLAYING FAVORITES

Favorite film:

Favorite scene:

Playing Favorites

Favorite TV program:

Favorite character:

PLAYING FAVORITES

Favorite piece of clothing:

Favorite room at home:

Favorite vice:

Favorite musical artist:

Favorite song:

Favorite novel:

Favorite children's book:

Favorite bedtime story:

Playing Favorites

Favorite rainy day activity:

Favorite sunny day activity:

Favorite physical activity:

Favorite cultural activity:

Favorite vacation destination:

Favorite sight:

FAVORITE PHOTOS

FAVORITE PHOTOS

Favorite Photos

heart

"*Out of the* MOUTHS *of babes and sucklings*
hast thou ORDAINED *strength.*"

–Psalms 8:2

Heart

O*f all the senses and abilities possessed by humans,*

there is no deeper truth than that understood by the heart.

While mothers already know this,

daughters learn to trust it.

HEART

Things I am passionate about, and why:

HEART

Things that make me sentimental, and why:

HEART

My greatest joy:

Heart

If words could express my love for you:

HEART

Things that make me angry:

HEART

Things that make me happy:

Heart

When my happy tears flow:

Heart

When my sad tears flow:

HEART

Pet peeves:

HEART

Personal heroes:

HEART

Most treasured possessions:

HEART

Things to be proud of:

A Picture's Worth

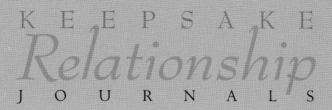

KEEPSAKE *Relationship* JOURNALS

Sophisticated, cloth-bound journals celebrate the moments and relationships that enrich our lives. An emotive music CD included.

FRIENDS FOR LIFE: Mother & Daughter Journal

HONOR & CHERISH: Wedding Journal & Planner

A LIFETIME OF MEMORIES: Baby Keepsake Journal

BEGINNINGS: Pregnancy Journal

TOGETHER FOREVER: Anniversary Journal

Look for these other journal series from Compass Labs:

• KEEPSAKE INSPIRATION COLLECTION: Heirloom-quality journals that accompany you on your spiritual journey. Thought-provoking prompts and an inspirational music CD are included to enhance your journaling experience.

• ACTIVE COLLECTION: Portable. Durable. Adventurous. Active journals add a take-along dimension to journaling for today's busy lifestyles. Theme-specific music CD included.

• EVOLUTION COLLECTION: Large–format workbooks serve as a personal coach as you reflect on a variety of life skills and events.

Compass journals – Helping to make sure
your memories don't get left behind!

Editor: Tom Lieberman
Art Director: Gail Onstad
Production Designer: Westerberg Design, Inc.
Photography: Ann Marsden
Bill Ling/FPG